*Mission in the Marianas*

A Publication from the James Ford Bell Library
at the University of Minnesota

# MISSION

## IN THE

# MARIANAS

An Account of
Father Diego Luis de Sanvítores
and His Companions
1669-1670

»»»»»»»»»»»»»»»»»»»»»»»»»»»»»»»»»»»»»»»»»»»»»»»»

*translated, with commentary,*

*by Ward Barrett*

University of Minnesota Press
Minneapolis

Copyright © 1975 by the University of Minnesota.
All rights reserved.
Printed in the United States of America
at
Napco Graphic Arts, Inc., New Berlin, Wisconsin.
Published in Canada by Burns & MacEachern Limited,
Don Mills, Ontario

*Library of Congress Catalog Card Number 74-27258*

*ISBN  0-8166-0747-8*

# PREFACE

t no other time in our history than is the case today have more Americans had more direct and more varied experience with people of foreign cultures—in missions, as we call them, of technical, military, and institutional aid, in the Peace Corps, in serving multinational businesses, through formal study, or as more or less observant tourists. Perhaps the number of foreigners who now know one or another Pacific language exceeds the total number of foreigners in all past eras who have known the same languages. If we pass beyond knowledge, uncertain though it may be, to its application, however crude, it may be true that more foreigners have tried in the last twenty-five years to change Pacific societies than did so in all the rest of their history. It is our custom to use "economic development" to describe the broad range of effects of these recent and intensified relationships and efforts, and we have allowed that term to swell in meaning to include all human activities, to encompass changes at all stages of the life cycle, from reproduction to education, from ways of working to alteration of burial rites in the name of public good health.

Perhaps the world has never seen a more inclusive, restlessly wide-reaching, secular doctrine than this one. But it is useful to remind ourselves that similarly conscious and comprehensive efforts to alter foreign cultures were launched in the past, with the important difference that a stronger and more explicitly religious charge was at the core of many earlier "missions," such as the one described in this brief report from the Marianas. Some today regard themselves as more sophisticated—and how useful here is the lingering ambiguity of this word of shifted meaning—in their dealings with foreigners than were those well-intentioned men of God, among the best educated of their time, who went to the Marianas in the late seventeenth century to save the heathen. Others say that only the words have changed, that the results of good intentions are at least as important as the intentions themselves.

I have come to owe so much touching on these themes to diverse conversations with many colleagues at the University of Minnesota that I shall not mention all their names: when a topic engrosses so many others as to become an envelope of the times, what is not pertinent? But I owe special thanks to Professor Ernest Greene, emeritus of Dartmouth College, whose close attention to the meanings of Spanish and English words saved me from many an error in the part of the translation that he had time to read; and to my good neighbor Katherine Greene Lewis, whose suggestions and searching questions contributed to the clarification of this text.

The original of this translation (*Noticia de los Progressos de Nuestra Santa Fe, en las Islas Marianas, llamadas antes de los Ladrones . . .*) is in the James Ford Bell Library of the University of Minnesota. In making this translation available the library is continuing the tradition of sharing its resources with the public. To the readers who wish to know more about the history of the Marianas, I recommend highly the interesting work of Paul Carano and Pedro C. Sanchez, *A Complete History of Guam* (Rutland, Vermont, and Tokyo, 1964).

If among our principal tasks are to preserve, to examine,

and to present the record as best we can, then all of us are indebted to Mariano Cuevas, S.J., for his presentation of the late-sixteenth-century sailing chart on which the reproduction below is based. This was published by him in color in his *Monje y Marino: La vida y los tiempos de Fray Andrés de Urdaneta* (Mexico City, 1943, facing p. 264), with the wish that it might be better known than has turned out to be the case; perhaps this latest representation of a beautiful map, now destroyed, will lead more readers to study his gift to us.

Ward Barrett

St. Paul, Minnesota
January 1975

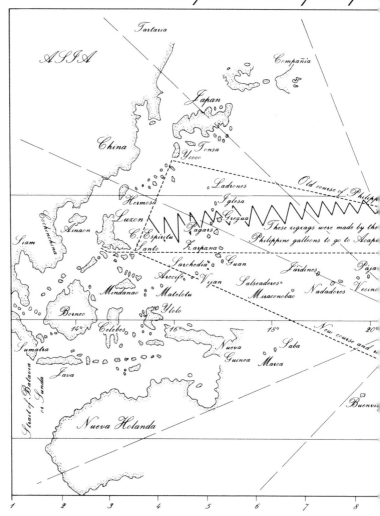

*Old and new courses from the Port of Acapulco*

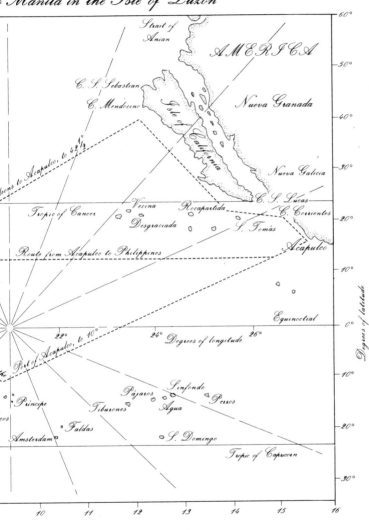

Strait of Anian

*AMERICA*

C. S. Sebastian

C. Mendocino

*Isle of California*

*Nueva Granada*

*Nueva Galicia*

Galeons to Acapulco, to 42½°

Vecina

Recapartida

C. S. Lucas

C. Corrientes

Tropic of Cancer

Desgraciada

S. Tomás

Acapulco

Route from Acapulco to Philippines

Equinoctial

Degrees of latitude

22°, to 10°

24° Degrees of longitude 26°

Port of Acapulco, to 10°

Sinfondo

The

Pájaros

Perros

Príncipe

Tiburones

Agua

Cocos

Faldas

Amsterdam

S. Domingo

Tropic of Capricorn

10      11      12      13      14      15      16

60°

50°

40°

30°

20°

10°

0°

10°

20°

30°

# CONTENTS

*Prologue*

he source of this translation is a printed quarto pamphlet of twenty-eight pages, published in Madrid about 1671. The pamphlet contains information about the culture of the people of the Marianas Islands and a report of events of the second year of the Jesuit mission there, a mission begun in June of 1668. Its pages ring and echo with the rhetoric of the missionaries who with single-minded devotion both followed and preceded the sword in the Spanish Empire: these were men never satisfied that they had saved enough souls for God and Church, zealously eager to spread the Word to the limits of the earth, to set more and more souls on the way to heaven through a truly Universal Church. It was the fervid zeal of one of their number, Diego Luis de Sanvítores, that altered so greatly the lives of the people of the Marianas and led to his celebrated martyrdom there in 1672.

Sanvítores was born in Burgos in 1627, scion of one of the most illustrious families of the region. His mother's family claimed descent from a relative of El Cid, and his father, also of distinguished lineage and a member of the Order of Santiago, served in the councils of the King of Spain. The son early eschewed the material rewards his birth might bring; Charles Le Gobien, a contemporary

Jesuit historian, wrote of him that "he was more distinguished by virtue than by his birth, although he belonged to one of the most illustrious families of Burgos." The virtue exhibited itself when he reached thirteen and decided to become a Jesuit against the wishes of his father, who also opposed his later decision to become a missionary. The willingness of members of the order to accept him at so tender an age may testify as much to his intellectual abilities as to his religious zeal.

Sanvítores shared with many other Jesuits of his time a passionate wish to be a missionary in China or Japan, the place of martyrdom of so many Christians earlier in the seventeenth century, but he was sent instead to the Philippines. Sanvítores took the only route, west from Spain via Mexico. After an Atlantic crossing and an interlude of highly successful preaching in Mexico, he finally left Acapulco in 1662 in the Manila galleon, which sometimes called at the Marianas on its way to the Philippines: a course set nearly due westward from Acapulco made these islands the first landfall for the galleon, the only quasi-regular, official means of reaching Manila from the New World.[1] In 1662, the galleon did call at Guam, largest of the Marianas, where Sanvítores reflected sadly on the miserable fate of the inhabitants: uninstructed in Christianity, they could never enter heaven. Their plight determined him to become the first missionary to the Marianas, then called by the name given them by Magellan, the Isles of Thieves.

During six years of missionary toil in the Philippines he never lost sight of this goal, tirelessly attempting to convince ecclesiastical and royal officials both in the Philippines and in Spain of the worth of his plan. The local officials entered numerous objections, all expectable: there were many souls to save in the Philippines; there was no money; all the ships that had ever attempted to sail into

[1] Information about the Manila galleon is contained in William L. Schurz, *The Manila Galleon* (New York, 1939).

the trade winds from Manila to the Marianas had failed to reach their goal. Finally, after the intervention of the Jesuit confessor to the Queen of Spain, he obtained permission in 1665 to found a Marianas mission; the prominent position of his father at the court may also have helped his effort. Thus the Isles of Thieves came to be renamed the Marianas in honor of the Queen of Spain.

Sanvítores also received permission to return to Mexico to raise money for the mission, as well as to get money released there by royal order to establish it. He left the Philippines in August 1667 and was very warmly received on his return to Mexico, where his inspired preaching had been fondly remembered. With gifts of money and devotional objects, he sailed from Acapulco in April 1668, accompanied by four priests, one student for the priesthood, and thirty laymen to act as catechists, finally stepping ashore on Guam after nearly three months at sea.[2]

He had wasted no time on the voyage, spending many hours working on a grammar of the language of the Marianos.[3] Not only was Sanvítores an inspired preacher of the Gospel; he also had an extraordinary flair for learning exotic languages. He had learned Tagalog so quickly in the Philippines and had used it there so effectively that some of his fellow missionaries regarded his achievement as miraculous. In working to master the language of the Marianos while on the long sea voyage out of Acapulco, he was helped by a Tagalog who had spent seventeen years in the Marianas after surviving the wreck of the galleon *Concepción* there in 1638. The grammar that San-

[2] Diego Luis de Sanvítores, *Memorial que . . . remitio a la Congregacion . . . [de] San Francisco Xavier de la Cuidad de Mexico, pidiendo le ayuden . . .* (Mexico City, 1669); this printed pamphlet indicates the special relationship Sanvítores had developed with this important congregation, some of whose members now gave him support. One of its members was the influential Conde de Santiago Calimaya, who was also *Adelantado* of the Marianas and the missions at this time, and the viceroy was its patron.

[3] Throughout this work, I will use the word used by the Spanish, Marianos, to describe the people of the Marianas.

vítores prepared with his help was, of course, the first
written grammar of the language. He learned the language so well that in his first two days on Guam he wel-
comed fifty converts into the Faith; he sent the grammar
on with the ship so that others might prepare themselves
to speak the language before they arrived in the islands.[4]

Sanvítores died on April 2, 1672. He was traveling to
Agana on the coast of Guam when, early in the morning,
he stopped at a house where he found an unbaptized
baby, which he insisted on baptizing against the wishes of
the father. Helped by a male friend, the father killed both
Sanvítores and his lay companion with club and spear,
weighted the bodies with rocks, and threw them into the
sea. Within a short time, several accounts of his life that
incorporated a description of the event of his martyrdom
were published and enjoyed great popularity. His life and
death had become exemplary.[5]

The pamphlet translated here is one of four reports cov-
ering the first two years of the Marianas mission: a short
and a long version were published for each year, and this
is the shorter report of the second year, slightly more than
half as long as the other. The compiler was Andrés de
Ledesma, procurator of the Society of Jesus in the Philippines, who selected material for the pamphlets from the
letters written by Sanvítores and his companions, and

[4] E. J. Burrus, "Sanvítores' Grammar and Catechism in the Mariana (or Chamorro) Language (1668)," Anthropos, 49:934–939
(1954).

[5] I have used several sources to compile this short biographical
sketch of Sanvítores: there is useful information in Charles Le
Gobien, Histoire des isles Marianes . . . (Paris, 1700); Francesco
Garzia (in fact, Francisco García), Istoria della conversione alla
nostra Santa Fede Dell' ISOLE MARIANE . . . translated by
Ambrosio Ortiz (Naples, 1686); Burrus, in Anthropos, 49:934–960;
H. de la Costa, The Jesuits in the Philippines (Cambridge, Mass.,
1961), pp. 455–456. The García and Le Gobien works contain
eulogies of Sanvítores; others are listed in Robert Streit, Missionsliteratur von Australien und Ozeanien, 1525–1950, vol. 21 of Biblio-
theca Missionum (Freiburg, 1955), pp. 35–47.

who was in Spain to recruit missionaries at the time of the printing of at least the short report of the first year.[6]

The printing of the Jesuit reports may or may not have aided Ledesma's efforts to recruit missionaries, but, more importantly, they are very similar to those documents issuing originally from New France and known, in printed form, as *The Jesuit Relations*. These were published from 1632 to 1672 as an annual series of reports from the superiors of Jesuit missions there to their provincials in France. Although the title *The Jesuit Relations* has exclusive application to the French series, it is obvious that the short series of four reports from the Marianas conforms in intent and form to the French model. The Jesuit reports from the Marianas Islands had a regrettably short history, but would have been terminated in any case by an edict of the pope in 1672 forbidding publication of such works.

There were several motives for publishing accounts such as these. They were intended for popular use—in fact, they were best sellers of their day—and were printed in relatively large numbers, some of the Canadian reports receiving two or three printings in France alone. The published accounts helped to advertise the work of the missions and attract donations for their support, donations made necessary by the fact that there was no general fund of the Jesuit Order through which the missions were financed. It was, of course, the policy that they should be self-supporting that led Sanvítores to seek donations in Mexico before going to the Marianas to found his mission. Lawrence Wroth tells us that the series of *Jesuit Relations* from New France were also a source of national pride, since they were the only chronicle of French imperial expansion that was regularly published. They were of

[6] Ledesma's name does not appear on the pamphlet, but Streit attributes all four pamphlets to him (*Missionsliteratur*, pp. 39–40). Francisco Zambrano, *Diccionario Bio-bibliográfico de la Compañía de Jesús en México* (Mexico City, 1961–1970), vol. 8, pp. 509–510, shows that Ledesma left Vera Cruz for Spain in 1668 and was in Spain in at least 1669.

interest to French merchants, members of chartered companies, colonial officials, and politicians in the mother country, as well as those with simple human curiosity about other lands and ways. Similar groups and motives were intended to be satisfied in Spain by the publication of the series from the Marianas and appeals to imperial glory and dominion appear in many places in this example.[7]

As things turned out, whether because of the published chronicles or not, the Spanish Jesuit missions and especially those of the Marianas attracted a benefactress who provided gifts and money on a massive and unprecedented scale, in addition to political assistance, thus taking over from the bankrupt Spanish Crown much of the support of the missions. The "Mother of the Missions," as she came to be called, was María Guadalupe de Lencastre, Duchess of Aveiro, Arcos, and Maqueda. Born in Lisbon on January 11, 1630, a descendant of John of Gaunt, she was one of the highest nobility in Portugal. At the age of thirty-five, she married the Spanish Duke of Arcos, two years after moving to Spain because her eldest brother had been charged with treason in Portugal. She died in 1715 and was buried at the shrine of Guadalupe in Estremadura.

In the course of her long life of eighty-five years the palace of the "Mother of the Missions" in Madrid became one of the principal centers of geographical and ethnographical information in Europe. To it came missionaries from many parts of Europe, and in and out flowed the enormous correspondence the duchess maintained with them while they were in the field. This was a salon very

[7] A useful description of *The Jesuit Relations* of New France is found in C. W. Colby, "*The Jesuit Relations*," *American Historical Review*, 7:36–55 (1901). The collection of the Bell Library is described in Frank Walter and Virginia Doneghy, *Jesuit Relations and Other Americana in the Library of James F. Bell* (Minneapolis, 1950). Other information is given in Lawrence Wroth's introduction to James McCoy, *Jesuit Relations of Canada, 1632–1673* (Paris, 1937), pp. iii–xv.

different from the better known ones of the eighteenth century, combining as it did deep religious feeling with perhaps as much intellectual depth and range as the times allowed. The duchess supported and encouraged the writing and publication of many learned works which, as a corpus, spanned the intellectual interests of the day. Her linguistic talent was considerable, and she is also said to have been a fair painter. This remarkable woman is virtually unknown today, her life and work never given the examination they so surely deserve.

The Marianas gained her special interest and favor, yet it is not clear why this should have occurred. Was it because, as Sanvítores never tired of insisting, there was special virtue in helping the most obscure, backward, and poor, and she wanted to achieve that virtue? Her interest may have been politic, inasmuch as the islands had been renamed for Mariana of Austria, Queen of Spain, and it would not have been imprudent for a Portuguese duchess living in Spain to take an interest in a namesake of so difficult a ruler. Whatever her motive, the duchess greatly assisted the missions in the Marianas while attempting to make good her vow to build as many churches as Elizabeth of England had destroyed.[8]

This translation is meant to retain as much as possible of the style and flavor of the original. The sentences are long, perhaps awkwardly so to those unfamiliar with written Spanish of the sixteenth and seventeenth centuries.

---

[8] The only biographical sketch of the duchess that I have found is in E. J. Burrus, *Father Kino Writes to the Duchess* (Rome, 1965), pp. v–vi. Her vow to build churches to compensate for the deeds of Queen Elizabeth supplies an interesting parallel to what was claimed for Cortés: that he had brought, through the Conquest of Mexico, as many people into the Catholic Church as Luther had taken away. The House of Aveiro was extinguished in Portugal by the minister Pombal on charges of treason in the eighteenth century: he ordered some of the family to be executed, the name forgotten, the palace razed, and its site strewn with salt.

In the Spanish of those days, long, complex, and at times nearly hopelessly entangled sentences were a standard mark of prose. English, by contrast, never experienced a phase dominated by construction of this sort. I have broken some of the original sentences into shorter ones where the thoughts could be separated without damage to their sense. But most remain as they were written, winding and meandering in leisurely fashion across the pages in a manner pleasingly different from that of modern prose.

*The Translation*

✠

# NOTICIA
## DE LOS PROGRESSOS

DE NVESTRA SANTA FE , EN
las Islas Marianas, llamadas antes de los Ladrones, y de el fruto que han hecho en ellas
el Padre Diego Luis de Sanvitores , y sus
Compañeros, de la Compañia de Iesvs, desde 15. de Mayo de 1669. hasta 28. de Abril
de 1670. sacada de las cartas, que ha escrito
el Padre Diego Luis de Sanvitores , y sus
Compañeros.

N la Relacion passada se diò noticia de las ca-
lidades de las Islas Marianas, de las costum-
bres de sus naturales, y de el fruto admirable,
que se dignò obrar la mano poderosa de Dios,
por medio de los Religiosos de la Compañia
de Iesvs, en el primer año de su Mission, desde 16. de Iunio de 1668. hasta 15. de Mayo de 669. con al-
gunos milagros, que obrò el Señor, para introducir la Fè en
aquellas Regiones, donde aun no se auia oìdo el Evangelio.
Aora, prosiguiendo esta Relacion, daremos noticia breve
(no qual pedia la dignidad de la materia, que necessitaua de
mas dilatado estilo, sino qual se deue à la ocupaciò, y grauis-
simos negocios de las altas personas, à quien esta Relacion se

A       di-

*News of the progress of our Holy Faith
in the Marianas Islands, formerly called the
Isles of Thieves, and of the work that
Father Diego Luis de Sanvitores and his
companions of the Company of Jesus
have done there, from the fifteenth
of May 1669 until the twenty-eighth of
April 1670, taken from their letters.*

n the previous report we described the resources of the Marianas Islands, the customs of their natives, and the admirable achievement worked by the almighty hand of God through the members of the Company of Jesus in the first year of their mission, from the sixteenth of June of 1668 until the fifteenth of May of 1669, together with some miracles worked by the Lord to introduce the Faith into those lands, where the Gospel had never been heard. Now, continuing this account, we will give a brief description (not appropriate to the dignity of the subject, which requires a more leisurely style than that permitted by the burdens and most important preoccupations of the distinguished persons to whom this account is directed) of the accomplishments that the Faith has enjoyed in its second year there, including first both curious and necessary news about the resources of the land and the customs, errors, and superstitions of the people of the Marianas, recently found out and not included in the first account.

The Marianas Islands, until now unfamiliar and unlit by the light of the Holy Gospel, are thirteen in number.

13

There are two other islands,[1] well populated and three days' journey to the south, besides those innumerable islands that continue to the Austral land, formerly unknown; and on the north side they continue as far as Japan which, according to early accounts and voyages, is about six days' journey from the island of San Lorenzo, the last that can be reached with the vessels of these parts; a prosperous and easy route, if there were larger ships to carry the Faith to those islands, consecrated by the Apostolic feet of Saint Francis Xavier and wetted by his sweat and blood, which is like seed under frost, only waiting for the sun to show itself there to fill the land with the flowers and fruits of Christianity. May God grant that it happens in the time of our Great Monarch Charles the Second, that he may boast that it was he who, in God's Glory, restored the Faith to the kingdom, wherefrom idolatry has banished it, and he who put Christ into possession of that far-flung empire that the Devil holds unjustly through usurpation. The thirteen islands, where until now the Gospel has been preached, lie between thirteen and twenty-two degrees, a little more or less, of north latitude; beginning in the south-southeast, they end in the north-northeast, after forming the figure of a half-moon, and so making a fitting pedestal for the feet of most Holy Mary, to whom they are dedicated. Some islands are very little distant from others, and the most distant is only a day's journey, so that their inhabitants traffic amongst themselves and speak a single tongue.

There have been found in these islands some harbors

---

[1] The reference to two other well-populated islands to the south is unclear. The Marianas are a well-defined group of thirteen islands arranged in a sublinear pattern between about thirteen and twenty-two degrees, as the writer clearly stated. Perhaps he was making reference to the Hondius map of 1628, which shows, however, three rather than two islands just south of Guam (Gugehan on his map); they extend south to about ten degrees north and are out of place there. Gerardus Mercator, *Atlas sive Cosmographicae Meditationes de fabrica mundi* . . . (Amsterdam, 1628), vol. 2, pp. 678–679.

suitable to provide berth for ships going to Mexico or returning from Mexico to the Philippines, owing to the search made by Don Juan de Santa Cruz, captain of these islands, by order of the governor of the Philippines. The island of Guam, now San Juan, the first where the Faith entered and where the Fathers of the Company of Jesus disembarked in the year 1668, has seven harbors, the one of San Antonio being on the west side, in front of a village which the natives called Hati, at which harbor there are two good rivers for a watering stop. Another port, where the Hollander[2] stayed in past years for about three months to beach and clean three ships, is about half a league from a point that divides the inlet of San Antonio, toward the south side and in front of a village that is called Humatag in their language; it has a very good river, from which the Hollander took on water. Continuing along this south side, one finds the third port, three leagues distant and in front of a village called Habadian, which has some shelter from the west and more from the north, but lacks a river. Continuing another three leagues toward the east, there are two coves separated by a point of land, with two rivers: the first in front of a village they call Pigpug, and the second in front of another village called Irig, more to the east; they have good shelter from other winds. Leaving the harbor of San Antonio, which we spoke of before, and moving a musket shot away to the north side,

[2] At least three Dutch fleets had stopped in the Marianas in the early seventeenth century, the first two for two days only (Van Noort's ships were there in 1600 and Spilbergen's were there in 1616). The Nassau fleet arrived on January 25, 1625, at the Marianas, but departed on February 11 for the Moluccas. James Burney, *A Chronological History of the Voyages and Discoveries in the South Seas . . .* (London, 1803–1817), vol. 2, pp. 225–226, 350; vol. 3, pp. 33–34. According to Andrew Sharp, *The Discovery of the Pacific Islands* (Oxford, 1970), p. 86, Maerten Gerritszoon Vries (a captain of the Dutch East India Company) was in the Marianas in about 1645. Scarcely any details of the voyage are known, and Sharp does not say how many ships were under Vries's command; in other words, the "Hollander" and his ships referred to in this pamphlet do not resemble any well-known fleet and its commander.

there is another harbor in front of the village they call
Taragrichan, with good water from two rivers alongside,
and the same shelter from the winds as the harbor of San
Antonio. Continuing more to the north, near the village
of San Ignacio de Agadña and the site of the principal
church and house of the Fathers of the Company, and in
front of a rocky headland that faces west-northwest, there
is a very good bottom of sand at a depth of eighteen
fathoms and only a harquebus shot from said headland;
and two musket shots from the headland is bottom at ten
fathoms; and entering a harquebus shot further toward
land, there is bottom at twenty-two fathoms. A very good
river debouches in the middle of the cove; it is sheltered
from all winds, and seems to be the best and most suitable
harbor on this island of San Juan.[3] In the island of Zarpana, now Santa Ana, which the natives call Roba, there
is a harbor wherein the Hollander anchored with the three
ships mentioned above; it is in front of a village that they
call Socanrago, now San Pedro, and faces northwest. One
league to the south there is another anchorage with a good
bottom and shelter from all winds. In the island of Saypan, now called Saint Joseph, and commonly the Great
Zarpan,[4] there is a good harbor whose mouth faces east,
from which, and even more from other winds, it is pro-
tected by a principal headland of the island that faces
southeast; the anchorage is in front of a village they call
Raurau. In the isles farther north, which they call Isle of
Pani and Isle of the Volcanoes, the Father of the Com-

―――――――――――――――――――――――――――――――――――――――――――――――――

[3] In spite of all the searching for harbors, and the praise lavished
on those that were found, there are no really good harbors in the
Marianas; galleons could not come to the shore at Agana (this was
one of the reasons why the commanders did not always stop) but
had to stand some distance off, and at present there is only a
small craft harbor there. The principal port, Apra Harbor, about
five kilometers west and southwest of Agana, is afforded only
partial protection by a long low island and an extensive breakwater.

[4] Saipan and Rota are here linked by similar names for a reason
that is not clear, with Saipan called the Great Zarpan, Rota simply
Zarpana. Zarpan may be a variant of Saipan.

Vrac, Isle deserte

Maug, ou Tunas
dite Isle de St Laurent

Assonsong, ou l'Isle
de l'Assomption

Agrigan, ou l'Isle
de St François Xavier

Pagon, ou l'Isle
de St Ignace

Amalagan, ou l'Isle
de la Conception

Guguan, ou l'Isle
de St Philippe

Sarigan, ou l'Isle
de St Charles

Anatajan, ou l'Isle
de St Ioachim

Saypan, ou l'Isle
de St Ioseph

Tinian, ou l'Isle de
Buena Vista Mariana

Aguiguan, ou l'Isle
de St Ange

Zarpane, ou Rota
dite l'Isle de St Anne

Guahan ou Guan,
dite l'Isle de St Iean

ARCHIPEL DE ST. LAZARE

LES ISLES MARIANES

pany and minister to those islands writes that there are some good harbors, especially one that is on the west side of the Isle of Agrigan, now Saint Francis Xavier, and about fifteen leagues north of the Isle of the Volcanoes, which is very well able to provide berth for the galleons when they come from Manila. With so many harbors, the help needed by the ministers who work in these islands is easy to give.

The people of the Marianas say, by tradition passed from father to son and without other history than their memory, that people came from the south to populate these islands, and that they have the same origin as the Tagalog; and their argument is supported not a little by the similarity in their tinting of their teeth, and by the similarity in their languages and mode of government. When, or for what reason, they came to these islands is unknown; some think that some tempest drove them here from the nearest islands of the Philippines, as has happened to others who have been driven from these islands to the islands of the Visayas. There are writers who trace the origin of the Marianos to the Egyptians, in accord with the idea that Gómara says (in his *General History of the Indies*, chapter 22) was set forth by Magellan, when he arrived in these islands in the year 1521. Others (as Father Colin says in his *India Sacra*, book 3, note 104) place their origin in Japan, and this origin is very plausible, at least for the people of the northernmost islands. But to detain ourselves in ascertaining the ancestry of some naked savages is to imitate those who commit to memory their genealogies, priding themselves as much on their nobility as if they were children of the sun.[5]

[5] Like other Europeans, the Spanish had great interest and difficulty in ascertaining the origins of the American Indians. Lee Huddleston, *Origins of the American Indians: European Concepts, 1492–1729* (Austin, 1967). Despite the difficulty, the tradition of attempting to determine origins remained very important, and the origins of the Pacific islanders continue to interest scholars. Although the Marianas are often placed in the Micronesian culture realm, they are in many respects quite different from the rest of

These thirteen islands have a healthful clime and a temperate sky, lacking the excessive heat and cold and earthquakes that occur in other islands of this archipelago.[6] Their waters are healthful, and so abundant in the principal island of San Juan that in its thirty-five or forty leagues of shoreline there are more than thirty rivers, some of copious flow and well stocked with fish, especially eels. These islands do not know snake, or cayman, or other venomous animal. There is a great abundance of coconut groves and goodly number of other trees, especially *palo maría*,[7] of which they make their boats. They live in villages of ten, twenty, thirty, and some of sixty, eighty, and more than one hundred houses, which they make of wood, with many on stone pillars, roofing them with coconut leaves, most curiously plaited. Especially do they take great pains in building their sleeping houses, or pavilions, which they hang with mats and with curtains of the same. The ordinary food of this people is fish, which they prize highly; for bread they use the fruit of

this group and the relationship of the language, called Chamorro, to Micronesian languages is "quite remote," according to Donald Topping, *Spoken Chamorro: An Intensive Language Course* . . . (Honolulu, 1969), p. xi. Some of the scholars who are still debating the means by which people reached the Pacific islands emphasize the importance of drift voyages. Others cite the great virtuosity of traditional navigators. See, for example, Thomas Gladwin, *East Is a Big Bird: Navigation and Logic on Puluwat Atoll* (Cambridge, Mass., 1970); M. Levison, R. G. Ward, and J. W. Webb, *A Computer Simulation of the Settlement of Polynesia* (Minneapolis, 1973).

[6] This is the first reference of several in the pamphlet to the conception of a vast archipelago of islands extending from at least Japan south to Australia, or Tierra Australis, the latter being referred to later as "the reputed fifth part of the world."

[7] *Palo maría* is identified as *Callophyllum inophyllum* by William Safford in *The Useful Plants of the Island of Guam* . . . vol. 9 of Smithsonian Institution (U.S. National Museum), *Contributions from the U.S. National Herbarium* (Washington, D.C., 1905), pp. 208–209. It is a common near-shore tree of the Pacific and Indian oceans; "its wood is hard, strong, cross-grained, and very hard to split. . . . It is durable in water, but is so rigid that it cannot be bent."

a tree, so delicious that even those recently arrived from
Spain do not miss wheaten bread; and in the seasons when
this fruit cannot be had, they serve some roots as bread,
similar to those of the Philippines, called *gauis, vuis,* and
*tuguis.*[8] In their most ceremonious gatherings and solemn
feasts, they eat rice, of which there is goodly abundance.[9]
At their meals, they are very moderate; and at the feasts
there are no excesses in eating or drinking, nor do they
use any liquor that causes drunkenness, a thing that has
impeded the introduction of the Faith and Christian customs into so many lands. Their celebration on these occasions is nothing more than recounting their histories,
wrestling, and throwing spears; and during these entertainments they pass about for refreshments some cakes of
*morisqueta, tamales,* fishes, coconuts, plantains, sugarcane,
and, in place of chocolate, a drink of *atole,* rice and grated
coconut.[10] The women have their special feasts, for which
they adorn themselves with ornaments on their foreheads,
some of flowers like jasmine, and some of valued trinkets
and tortoiseshells, hung from a string of red shells that
are prized among them as are pearls among us, and of

[8] The fruit of the tree is undoubtedly breadfruit; gauis, vuis, and
tuguis are, respectively, *Colocasia esculentum* (taro), *Dioscorea
fasciculata* (kidney yam), and probably *Dioscorea alata*; the popular name given here for one of the latter (*vuis*) is probably a misprint for some variant of *ubi,* one of the names used in the Philippines. The last two are both cultivated yams. *Gauis* may be a
misprint for some variant of *gavo,* the name applied to taro in the
Philippines. *Ibid.,* pp. 206–208, 259–260. A recent flora of Guam
uses somewhat different nomenclature; see B. C. Stone, *The Flora
of Guam,* vol. 6 (1970) of *Micronesica: Journal of the University
of Guam* (659 pages).

[9] The growing and eating of rice is one feature that sets the culture of the Marianos apart from Micronesian culture and makes it
closer to that of the Philippines.

[10] It is interesting that the cuisine of Mexico provides a basis for
comparison by the use of the words *tamale, chocolate,* and *atole.*
The latter may have signified a gruel of rice and grated coconut.
*Morisqueta* is a word used in the Philippines to describe rice cooked
in water without salt, and served without condiments. *Enciclopedia
Universal Ilustrada Europeo-Americana* (Barcelona, 1905–1933),
vol. 26, p. 112.

which they make also some waistbands with which they gird themselves, hanging around them some small, well-formed coconuts on some string skirts made of tree roots, with which they finish their costume and adornment, and which seems more birdcage than dress. Twelve or thirteen join together to form a circle, remaining in one place, singing in verses their histories and antiquities, with point and harmony of three voices, sopranos, contraltos, and falsettos, and with the tenor taken by one of the principal men, who attend these entertainments; and they accompany the singing by movements of the hands, with which they flourish some half-moons in the right, and in the left some cases of bells and shells which serve them as castanets, and all this so rhythmically, and with slapping, and with actions so well suited to words that it causes no little admiration to see how quickly they learn the things they apply themselves to. The women wear their hair very long and tint it with diverse rinses to make it white, and color their teeth with blacking, and this they consider the major adornment of their beauty. The men do not let their hair grow, but shave all the head, leaving only a tuft or crown on the top of the head, no more than a finger long.

The most ordinary exercise of this people is to fish, build boats, and cultivate their gardens. Their customs are better than their nudity and lack of culture and government suggested, of which some has been written already, and now more shall be added. The people are generally pacific, as is seen in the small number of wars they have amongst themselves, and in spite of the absence of magistrates and the great independence some of them show toward others, and with no one recognizing a common head, except only in families, where the right to family leadership is respected by the rest. This head of the family owns the principal house and the best land; and, as in India, the rights are not inherited by the son of the deceased but by his brother or his nephew, who on assuming it changes his name and takes that of the founder or principal ascendant of his family, with such respect for and such distinctions of lineages, high, low, and medium, that one cannot but marvel at such vanity or curiousness in poor, naked people; which shows, as we have said, their descent from some very civilized nation, much concerned with nobility. One of the highest class, called by them *Chamorris*, will not marry the daughter of a plebeian, be her father ever so rich and he ever so poor and needy, as is said of the Japanese; and formerly the noble who married the daughter of a plebeian was killed by his relatives. The *Chamorris* have such low esteem for those of low lineage that they will allow them neither food nor drink nor approach to the noble houses, but away from those houses they give them what they ask. They use great courtesies amongst themselves, and the usual custom, on meeting and passing ahead of another, is to say to him: "A ti arimo" (which means "Permit me to kiss your feet"), and when one passes by another's house, betel is brought out to him and given to him if he wishes to chew it.[11]

They hate murderers so much, and cruel persons,[12] that they do not give them the honor that they had before; for this reason they do not honor, as had been the custom, some villages of the island of Saypan, because they committed some years ago cruel acts and are too much in-

---

[11] Early works emphasize strongly the markedly, perhaps rigidly, hierarchical nature of society in the Marianas. The Chamorris or Chamorros were the highest class, and modern usage of this term to include all the people of the Marianas would have been regarded as wholly erroneous and inappropriate by all early observers. There may be an interesting story to be found in tracing the shift in usage of this term, given that the sanctions regarding intermingling of the classes were so harsh. Le Gobien (*Histoire des isles Marianes*, p. 49) describes three classes: nobles (Chamorris) who "have the people in a condition one cannot imagine in Europe," the lowest class, and a vaguely defined intermediate group. Le Gobien (*ibid.*, p. 51) also notes that the Chamorris exchanged pleasantries while walking.

[12] Le Gobien added thieves to the list, and elaborated on the theme that Magellan had misnamed the islands: the Marianos simply and rapidly took a great fancy to anything made of iron (*ibid.*, p. 62).

clined to make spears, which are their principal arms, together with the sling and stones which they are accustomed to use with dexterity from a tender age. They form the spears from the bones of their fathers, with some points in two and three rows in the form of fishhooks, so that in spite of their easy entry it is very difficult to take them out. The married men do not traffic with many women, or concubines, but the bachelors have some public houses, where they live with every freedom and no subjection whatever to their parents. In marriage, the jealousy of the wives is so great that if they feel some disloyalty on the part of their spouses, they punish them in various ways. Sometimes the injured woman gathers the other women of the village and, carrying hats and spears, they go to the house of the adulterer, and if he has a garden, they root it up and destroy it; and they threaten to spear him, and finally cast him from his house. At other times the injured woman punishes her husband by leaving him, and then the relatives of the woman gather at the house of the husband, and take whatever possessions he has, leaving not even a spear or a mat on which to sleep; only the shell of the house is left, and even this at times they are accustomed to destroy and pull down; and this is an indispensable custom. For this reason the woman commands the house, nor can the husband arrange anything without her pleasure and approval; what is more, he cannot punish his children, for if a wife hears of this, she leaves the house and parts from him, and all the children follow her, without recognizing another father than he whom their mother next takes for a husband.[13]

---

[13] Le Gobien's discussion of the place of the husband makes him seem far more disadvantaged than even this description does. Le Gobien wrote, for example, that women could not be punished for adultery and a husband's only recourse was to punish the other man; that, on separating, the women lost nothing and the men everything; that this rule by women caused young men not to marry, and so explained the use of dormitories by young men who kept one or more girls in them. In addition, his description of the vengeance taken by women on adulterous males is far more detailed

They have many erroneous beliefs about the creation of the earth, and other things, as if they were blind persons, lacking all light and doctrine, and without polity or any culture of letters. They were persuaded that they were the only men in the world, and that there was no other land in it beside their own; but later, with the experience of seeing our galleons pass, and the Hollander's ships, they rejected this error, and persuaded themselves that there were many other lands and men. They fell into another error, equal or greater, which they incorporated into their traditions: that all lands and men and all things had their origins in their land, and that all had first come forth from a part of the island of Guam, which was first a man, and then a stone, which gave birth to all men, and from there they scattered to Spain, and other parts.[14] They add that when others parted from their people and origin they forgot their language, and thus persons of other nations know no language whatever and speak like lunatics, without understanding one another, not knowing what they speak; and thus the Marianos attribute to everyone else their own ignorance in not understanding the language of foreigners. They claim that our ships, passing by their islands, left them rats, flies, mosquitoes, and all their sicknesses. And they are correct in the matter of sickness, because after the ships have been in their islands

---

and graphic: the wronged woman gathered *all* the women of the village as an army, and with spear in hand and the hat or helmet of her husband on her head, she marched with them to the house to do battle; if the husband had made the mistake of being there, they attacked him, and the relatives of the wife saw the occasion as an opportunity to enrich themselves at his expense, on the pretext of taking revenge and observing an "indispensable custom" (*ibid.*, pp. 59–62). This enormous power of women sets the culture of the Marianos apart from the rest of Pacific island societies, but what is missing here, as elsewhere in this and other works, is any indication whether these rules applied to all the population or only to the Chamorris.

[14] Le Gobien renders this more clearly (*ibid.*, p. 63): the first man was made and then changed to a stone, from which issued forth all other men.

they find themselves with colds and other infirmities; and this is the reason why, in spite of their greediness for iron and other little things, while the ships are in the bay, they do not leave shore by day or night; exposed to sun, to the dew of night, and to other inclemencies of the sea, they continually cry out, so that most return hoarse and with other ailments to their houses.

Of the creation of the world, they say that Puntan (who must have been the first of men, and who was blown to these islands by some tempest) was a most ingenious man, who lived many years in some imaginary spaces that existed before heaven and earth were created. This good man, being about to die, and feeling pity for the men whom he was leaving without land to inhabit, or withal to sustain themselves, called a sister of his, who had been born like himself without father or mother, and, telling her of the benefit that he proposed to confer on mankind, gave her all his powers, so that when he died she might make from his chest and back heaven and earth; from his eyes sun and moon; the rainbow from his eyebrows, and likewise form the rest, keeping some correspondence of the lesser world to the greater, as the poets do every day:[15] without this all would have remained as symbol, and Writ and Gospel would not have come to pass. This they sing in some bad verses that they know by heart, and that cause more laughter than harmony; but with all this it does not happen that they give said Puntan or his sister any worship of public ceremony or invocation or appeal which would acknowledge their Divinity. These and other antique fables and deeds of their ancestors are related and

---

[15] The passage refers to the doctrine of correspondences, where an object may be taken as symbol of something else; earlier, for example, the writer applied it to the crescent shape of the island chain, a shape that made it a "fitting pedestal" for the feet of Mary, whose symbol is the crescent moon. This correspondence must have pleased both Queen Mariana and María Guadalupe de Lencastre. For more information, see E. M. W. Tillyard, *The Elizabethan World Picture* (New York, 1944).

sung at their celebrations by those who pride themselves on being learned, competing to see who may speak most couplets, without there being in them any other evidence of religion or sect, priests or Bonzos, apart from some tricksters called Macanas, who generally promise health, water, fish, and such good things by means of the invocation of the dead of Zazarraguan (for thus they call hell), whose skulls the Marianos keep in their houses, with no other altar, niche, or adornment than some little baskets in which they put the skulls around the house, without remembering them until it is time for the Macanas to ask the skulls for what they need. The Macanas, like all the Bonzos and priests of India, in praying to the dead, seek their own advantage through what the living give them, and not the advantage of the living. The Macanas and almost all others recognize that there is nothing to expect from the dead, and if perhaps they call upon the dead with great feeling, it is not so much because they might give them what they want as because the dead might thus not do them harm; because the Devil, in order to maintain by whatever means their respect and servile fear, generally appears to them in the form of their parents and ancestors to frighten and ill-treat them.

This is the most that the Devil has been able to obtain from these poor people—no temples, or sacrifices, or idols, or profession of any cult whatever—a fact that aids very much in introducing the Faith, if there are ministers to preach it, because it is easier to introduce a religion where there is none than to overthrow one to introduce another. This made the way much easier for the Apostle to the Indies, Saint Francis Xavier, in going to preach on the island of Mazacar [sic], and so he says in a letter: "That land is very ready to receive Christ, because in it there are no temples of idols, nor ministers who compel the people to venerate false gods."

Nonetheless, these people have some superstitions, especially when fishing, when they keep complete silence and observe long fasts, through fear of the Anitis, the souls of their ancestors, or to flatter them, so that the Anitis will not punish them by taking away the fish or frightening them in dreams, to which they give much credit. When someone dies, it is customary to put at his head a basket, thus inviting him to remain at home in that basket instead of the body he leaves, or so that he may have somewhere to rest when he comes from the other life to pay them a visit from the place of his abode, which they believe to be underground, where those generally rest who have died (from natural causes) and with some suffering for those who die unfortunately.[16] Others are in the habit of carrying the corpse of their deceased one, after it is anointed with fragrant oils, to the houses of their relatives, either so that the soul may remain in the house where it wishes, or so that if it returns to this world it will alight where it most pleases. In burials, the demonstrations of grief that they make are very peculiar, with many tears, fasts, and noises of conches; the mourning continues by custom for six, eight, and more days, in accordance with the affection and duty they had toward the person who has died. They pass this time with melancholy songs, gathered around a catafalque that they set up on the grave, or alongside it, adorning it with flowers, palms, seashells, and other things much esteemed by them. The mother of the dead person customarily cuts a lock of his hair from his head, to keep as a remembrance of her sorrow, and notes the nights that follow his death by knots on a cord that she wears around her neck.[17]

[16] Le Gobien (*Histoire des isles Marianes*, p. 66) put it differently: The destination of a soul did not depend on virtue or the lack of it in life, but rather on the nature of one's death. Those who died a natural death went to paradise, those who died violently went to Zazarraguan, a far less pleasant place.

[17] Le Gobien restricts the custom of cutting a lock of the hair of the deceased to the case of the death of an infant; he wrote that the "desolation" of a mother who lost an infant was "inconceivable," a most important point in light of the reason for the death of Sanvítores. It appeared that many of the infants who were baptized died shortly thereafter; although they may have been ill,

These touching demonstrations of grief are heightened on the death of a leader, or *Chamorri*, as they call a person of the highest class, and on the death of some famous matron; for besides their ordinary demonstrations, they strew the paths with some ropes of palm leaves, erect triumphal arches and other gloomy structures, destroy coconut trees, burn houses, pull boats to pieces, and raise their shredded sails before their houses as signs of their grief and suffering: and they add dirges to their songs that are as ingenious as they are deeply felt, and which show their sorrow even to the most rude and barbarous, saying with many tears: "In the future, life will be a burden to you, lacking him who was the life of everyone, lacking the sun of nobility, the moon that lighted you in the night of your ignorance, the star of all your achievements, the valor of your battles, the honor of your lineage, of your people, and of your land"; and in this way they continue until well into the night in praise of the deceased, whose grave they crown with oars, to show he was a celebrated fisherman, or with spears, as signs of the brave, or with oars and spears if he was both brave and a fisherman. Leaving other errors and superstitions which would take too long to tell, we shall pass to the achievement that God has deigned to work in these islands, by means of the Fathers of the Company of Jesus, and their lay companions, who help them as much as they can.

With the blessing of God, and of the most Holy Virgin Mary, patroness of these islands, and with the help of the King our Lord, and the Queen our Lady (may God keep

---

many of the Marianos believed that the baptism was the cause of death. And with good reason: Sanvítores wrote to the queen that in the first year more than 100 infants went to heaven "immediately" after being baptized (*ibid.*, p. 109); but he does not say whether they were baptized because they were seriously ill. This passage concerning funeral customs, like the one describing marriage customs, lacks the force of the same passage in Le Gobien, who wrote that no people were more eloquent in expressing grief occasioned by death, and that they might fast so long as to become unrecognizable.

them many and happy years, for the increase of their
Faith), the missions have continued with great success in
the eleven islands that were in part reduced to Christianity the first year, and in the following year there have
been added two islands further north, the special difficulty
of having to go to them in the small boats of this land
having been overcome. The Faith entered the twelfth
island, before called Assonson and now called Assump-
ción, the same day that the Queen of Angels entered
heaven in her glorious Assumption, and entered the thir-
teenth on the day of the Octave of San Lorenzo, the
seventeenth of August. This island was called Maug, and
now is called San Lorenzo, and is the farthest north one
can go toward Japan with the small boats of those islands,
until larger ships are sent, in which the Faith can sail
those seas for the happiness of as many islands as need
these fleets from which heaven hopes for the greatest
benefits.

Counting adults and children, 30,000 persons have been
baptized in these two first years in the thirteen islands,
by the mercy of the Lord and Lady of them, not counting
a large number of catechumens, who are preparing to
receive baptism. As many as 300 children of those baptized have died, taken by God to heaven, that they may
pray for the conversion of their parents and relatives.

Five churches have been built according to plan and all
dedicated with all solemnity to God, in honor and name
of the most Holy Virgin Mary our Lady. In them the
Holy Days and divine services are celebrated with the
greatest solemnity possible, and with the Royal Chapel of
Mary being filled with the music of the children of the
Marianas, who with several parts make a very agreeable
harmony to the ears of their teachers and much more to
the ears of God, who takes pleasure in the praises of
children, for they come from pure and innocent mouths.
The services of Holy Week are conducted with altar,
flagellation, confessions, and processions, and we are try-
ing to make the Marianos devoted to our holy ceremonies

and Christian customs. All the churches that may be built
in the future are intended to be consecrated to Most Holy
Mary, all distinguished by the titles of her festivities and
images of special devotion that are found in various parts
of the world; and because the Faith was born in these
islands under Mary, the Star of the Sea, it cannot fail to
grow much to the honor and glory of God; and since those
of the Christian religion are an increase of the worship of
this Queen, the Son will increase their numbers more, to
honor his Mother more. Those devoted to Mary, help in
the conversion of these souls with your prayers, if you
cannot with your words by preaching of the Gospel, so
that God may send to that vineyard the workers needed
for its cultivation, since for lack of workers as many souls
are lost as each day die in darkness, so that they may go to
complain to the Court of God about those who, having
knowledge, have no concern for the Glory of God and
use the light of knowledge to seek honors and wealth,
when they should employ it to light the way of those
who stumble and fall in the shadows of death, and to help
Christ in saving the souls that he redeemed with his Blood.

Of the zeal of the preachers who go about in those
parts, of the hardships they suffer, of the dangers that surround them always, one may say almost what Saint Paul
says of himself in the description of his toil and perils sent
to the Corinthians, in Epistle 2, chapter 11, "For they
encounter perils of waters, perils of thieves (as the Marianos used to be called), perils in the city, perils in the
wilderness, perils in the sea, perils among false brethren;
in weariness and painfulness, in watchings often, in hunger and thirst, in fastings often, in cold and nakedness,
beside those things that are without, that which cometh
upon me daily, the care of all the churches." For what
hunger and thirst will those men suffer who are accustomed ordinarily to nourish themselves with the roots of
trees or some wild fruit, and by the gift of some little fish,
drinking only water, never eating bread, or meat, or drinking wine? What hardships do they suffer who journey

endlessly from one town to the next, from one island to another on foot [sic], alone, poorly garbed, with little protection from cold and heat; sleeping where night finds them, on bare ground, or on branches; teaching the Christian Doctrine to dull children or some barbarous men; hunting, like Saint Francis Xavier, in the houses for children or the sick in order to baptize them, for the dead to bury, controversies to settle, enmities to pacify, the needy to succor, doing the duties of Fathers, Teachers, and Apostles? What hardships will those preachers suffer who are so poor in all things, without even paper for writing, as they say in a letter left unfinished for lack of paper, and who could not say Mass for lack of bread and wine, were it not for the great providence and zeal of our Lady the Queen, who ordered sent with royal munificence what was needed, and through the care of her zealous officials, as happened in the year of 1669, when Field Marshal Don Manuel de León, who went as governor to the Philippines, anchored on the fifteenth of June in the harbor of San Antonio of the island of Guam and gave them bread and wine for the Holy Sacrifice of the Mass, and various other things suitable for the good and increase of Christianity there? While we await the special favor and assistance of royal charity, ordered but not yet received, bountiful help is supplied by the charity of others, by the pious officials of Her Majesty in those provinces, and by the Venerable Congregation of San Francisco Xavier of Mexico, and especially by their elder brothers, the most excellent viceroys, with their liberality and alms. And finally, what perils surround those who are always menaced by death from sling stones, spears, and poisons, for wanting to baptize creatures many of whom think baptism is fatal for them, and when all preachers have been badly treated, some injured, one dead, and those alive freed from death many times only by miraculous providence? We could say much, were it proper to praise the living, but, leaving until their times the particulars of each one (apart from those concerning the blessed martyr Father Luis de Medina, which will be told in his life) we will tell now of one and another of the most important happenings of this past year.

It is worthwhile to know about the beginning and end of the war of the island of Tinian, called the Buenavista Mariana.[18] The Devil, jealous of the ease with which the Faith progressed in this island and of the peaceful possession whereby Jesus Christ reigned in it, inflamed the spirits of the natives, some against the others, in such a way that in a few days what had been a paradise burned in flaming quarrels, as much more difficult to smother as were the spirits of this island the most haughty, the most jealous of their honor, and the most insolent about their nobility to be found in all these islands. The war lasted four months with its stonings and spearings, with many of the highest princes of one and another side dead, with burning of houses, destruction of their gardens, and great disturbance to the evangelical seedbed; nor were the many means of prayers, promises, and threats that were taken, nor the miracles worked by God before their eyes, sufficient to quiet them; for a Father of the Company put himself between the warring camps when they were stoning one another, and with a cross in his hand exhorted them to peace, receiving on his person many stones that, on hitting him, fell straight to his feet, and caused him no harm whatever, as those of the same island have admitted. It seemed that this conflagration must consume all the works produced through so much labor by the Faith in this island, unless some means were found to extinguish it; but as Divine Providence rules over all things human, and will not abandon its own, so it helped in the greatest need and gave power to a remedy as only its power could. Some few seculars, who had accompanied the Fathers,

---

[18] Tinian was called the Buenavista Mariana because a vision of Mary appeared there in 1638 to a Mariano named Taga when the ship *Concepción* was wrecked nearby; he cared for some victims of the shipwreck, and at the time the war began Tinian was considered ripe for conversion (*ibid.*, pp. 77–78).

were encouraged to take into their charge this so difficult and risky task, accomplishing by force of arms what could not be done peaceably. They were ten, of whom only one was a Spaniard, called Juan de Santiago, a Biscayan and of very tender age, the rest being natives of the Philippines; and the captain of all was Don Juan de Santa Cruz. They had three muskets and a small fieldpiece. The latter had been left (as if reserved by God for such occasions) on the celebrated wreck in these islands of the ship *Concepción* in the year of 1638; it had been salvaged and was found by chance in a house on the island of Saypan, during a search for the head of an image of Our Lady that some said was in it.

This small company, armed more by confidence in Divine Power than supported by the strength and power of their firearms, tried to impose order on two armed camps; they put themselves between two groups of warriors who were on the point of assailing one another, and sent emissaries to one and the other, pleading for peace and promising that the side first to start fighting would receive its just punishment. The two camps became calm for some time, owing to the natural fear that they have of firearms, and sent continuously emissaries of peace from one to the other.

In memory and thanks to the Most Holy Virgin for the gift of peace, a hermitage was raised between the two camps and named Our Lady of Peace; and this served our side as a garrison[19] to keep that peace. For the two months that our soldiers were there, through the fear and respect that they had earned, the sallies and sorties of one and the other party were prevented. But as the souls of these natives are most inconsistent and shifting, after two months of peace fighting broke out because of one death off the battlefield caused by one side, and the burning of a village by the other; men of the latter moved surreptitiously on a path distant from our force and the Hermi-

---

[19] *Plaza de armas* in the original.

tage of the Peace. For having started the fight in spite of the pacts that had been made, and for having attacked our defense with the intent of taking the firearms, which were all they feared, our soldiers gave this latter side a sprinkling from our arms as they had promised, although very light; for our soldiers intended more to frighten than to kill these warriors, it being necessary that the Marianos learn that our arms were not all thunderous noise and thunder without lightning, as they had said until then. Which they learned sufficiently well, for one was dead and another wounded, the latter being the principal force behind this war, speared by a Pampango boy,[20] he being little more than twelve years and called Andrés de la Cruz. Another young Spaniard, a native of Mexico called Diego Bazán, wounded others with much valor, and Captain Don Juan de Santa Cruz, who discharged the duties of leader of said force, ordered and inspired all our soldiers, before which all the enemies were prostrate; they lacked both food and the will to make their hands fight or their feet flee, terrified by the thunderous noise of our arms, and even more by the death of their companions. This demonstration of the *Guirragos* (for so in that land do they call Spaniards and foreigners, by way of saying those from overseas) has been most convenient, for the fear that our arms have earned has been great, not only in this island but also in the neighboring islands, where the news arrived quickly and demonstrated that abuses committed against the laws of God and the rules of good behavior taught by the Fathers would not go unpunished, and that hostilities would be suppressed.

So great is the fear that our arms and soldiers have earned that when all the villages of the warring faction gathered together to attack Sungaron, where the Fathers of the Company have a church and house, because they

---

[20] Pampango was a province in the Philippines where the natives had been Christian almost from the beginning of Spanish domination.

heard that all our soldiers had gone (on an absence of four days to the island of Saypan), upon hearing before their intended attack upon the village that there remained two or three *Guirragos*, and one *pequi*, which is the same as firearm, they retired to the point, without daring to attack. From which one sees how useful it is to have on each island, if not in every village, men and arms sufficient to introduce so healthy a fear, as well as justice and government, not only paternal but also coercive and military; necessary here, as everywhere, to repress the sins, insults, and fighting that impede the preaching of the Holy Gospel. Although the war ended, not all the spirit of it that had been lit was extinguished, for there were not lacking some sparks of conflict between the natives as well as against our people, whom, it is suspected, they have tried many times to poison; but God has freed them from this and many other dangers, through the favor of the most Holy Virgin and the intercession of the great Apostle of the Indies, Saint Francis Xavier, to whom this victory is primarily attributed.

When the Devil saw undone his first plot in the island of Tinian, he began a second in two other adjacent islands, Saypan and Anatagon (which are now called San José and San Joaquín), by spreading again in them the rumor that the Chinese Idolater (as I wrote in the first account)[21] had earlier spread in these islands: that the holy baptism was fatal to man because the holy oil and water were mixed with poison, with which the Fathers intended to take the life of anyone they baptized, espe-

[21] The "Chinese Idolater," a man called Choco, was blown to the Marianas on a ship that was attempting to go from Manila to Ternate in 1648. Observing that there was no religion in the Marianas, he set himself up as a religious leader, the Marianos listening to his novelties with great pleasure. With the arrival of the missionaries, his position was threatened and he attempted to incite the Marianos to kill the Spanish. Le Gobien's version (*Histoire des isles Marianes*, pp. 89–120) of the first "war" and Choco's role in it was probably based on Sanvítores's first letter.

cially the children, who, being more delicate, could not resist its power.

Those who had given more credit to the calumny of the Chinese than to the preachers of the truth, awaited some suitable occasion to reveal the poison of their infidelity to the ministers of the Gospel; and thus the most fervent and blessed Father Luis de Medina, going about the island of Saypan on one of his continuous missions, preaching to the natives and searching with great solicitude and zeal for children and the sick to baptize, found the merited and desired prize of his labors, the crown of martyrdom, together with a layman called Hipólito de la Cruz, native of Visaya, companion no less in his crowning than in his toil and zeal; for two villages of the said island did unite together and spear them to death, in hatred of our Faith and of the holy baptism; so it appears from the declarations of seventeen witnesses and from the principal aggressor, a man named Poyo, who gave the deepest and mortal thrust to the blessed Father Luis de Medina; and the impious aggressors shouted as they thrust their spears, crying blasphemies against God and insults against the Father, excoriating him because he wanted to kill their children with baptismal water.

I do not intend here to foresee the judgment of the Apostolic See, to which I subject myself in all things and whose declaration I await, but rather to say only what one properly should. This Father, born in Málaga, was a priest of our Company, a most fervent and zealous preacher who, at thirty-three years of age (with fourteen in the Company and two years of preaching in the Marianas), and after achieving great works in these islands against innumerable hardships and the continuous threat of death, died for Christ in the village of Cao, in the island of Saypan. Of his life and death, with all the circumstances of his martyrdom, the discovery of his body, and his many and rare virtues, and the favors done him by the Lord and the Queen of Angels, Most Holy Mary, I shall write separately, for I cannot put them in this report without making it too long; and it would be unjust to be silent or to speak so casually the praises of one who has so merited them with his useful life and most blessed death.

Besides these two blessed martyrs who died in the second year of this mission, another, a native of Malabar named Lorenzo, died in the first year. He was one of the Christians who were left in these islands after the wreck of the ship *Concepción* in the year of 1638, and he joined the Fathers of the Company in tilling that land after they entered into it. He visited one of the villages of the island of Anatagon to see if there was some child or sick person to baptize and found the prize of his great zeal; for some hated him, as if he were a murderer of children, because they had lost a few days before a child who had recently been baptized, and they killed him with such great cruelty—not content with wounding him many times, but also putting out his eyes and burying him in a public cesspool—as to give clear witness of the hatred they bore toward the holy baptism.

If, as Saint León says, the blood of the martyrs is the seed of Christians, then the blood of three martyrs does promise a great harvest, for with their blood they have watered this land, already most blessed; thus may there be workers so fervent that they come to gather this harvest without fear of the death that waits for them with a crown of immortality. But none can lose spirit in the face of deaths so glorious; instead all must be encouraged and covet so great a blessing in the knowledge that such precious crowns are given free of cost. To those who leave their knowledge idle like the treasure of the misers, we can repeat sorrowfully what is written by Saint Francis Xavier —in a letter—from the depths of his heart: "Woe unto you, when so great a number of souls cannot enter heaven, but must descend to hell, through your fault and sloth."

Requests made by the missionaries of the Company of Jesus in the Marianas to Her Majesty the Queen, our

Lady, for the growth of the new Christianity of the Marianas Islands.

1. They ask for more workers, both to indoctrinate the thirteen islands that are converted to our Holy Faith and to proselytize the many others that remain in the darkness of death and heathenism in this range from the Austral land to Japan; for here it is, as Christ said to his disciples, that the harvest is great and the workers few; and we should cry tears of blood because so many descend to the inferno every day for want of anyone to show them the road to heaven, and because so many children lose their place in glory for want of preachers to baptize them. For this, Your Majesty is asked to give permission to the Fathers of the Company of Jesus who may be foreigners, yet subjects of your Crown, to come to these islands; because the provinces of Spain, for lack of subjects, cannot give as many as are necessary for this work of such great glory to our Lord. And in said foreign realms there may be many who are called by the Lord to this mission, but who remain chained by the shackles of respect and obedience to the commands of Your Majesty. The expenses of said preachers will be no more than the costs of the voyage to the islands and the costs of divine worship in them; their sustenance may be trusted to Divine Providence which, as it does not forget the birds of the air, so it will also give sufficient of the fruits of the earth to those who would do its tilling with the true vocation of evangelical missionaries.

2. The second thing they request is a good number of secular companions, of various abilities and skills that they may teach to the Marianos; and especially good Christians, so that with their example they may teach Christian customs and serve as *Canacápoles*,[22] thus making up for

---

[22] As used in Malabar, this term referred to a kind of lawyer or notary, or a kind of procurator of the Church. Antonio de Morais Silva, *Grande Dicionário da Língua Portuguesa*, 10th ed. (N.p., n.d.), vol. 2, p. 820. In the Marianas it was evidently applied to lay teachers who might perform baptisms in emergencies.

the lack of priests for baptisms of necessity and for teach-ing the children; and on the way introduce a Christian order and some form of government and justice, which are totally wanting in these lands and whose absence would be a very grave defect in any land of very old Christianity. It would be useful if these latter, in addition to the tools of their trades, were to carry firearms, which inspire special terror in those islands and are of great con-venience because, although the Gospel entered unarmed into these islands, as a rule of peace and charity, in order to maintain itself in them and progress easily it needs to go surrounded by arms, as the Ark of the Testament of the Armies of God went, not so much to injure as to excite fear; and because if they lack fear and a coercive form of government they will dare greater insults than until now have been experienced and will kill all the preachers, as they have attempted to do at times, and, although for the preachers it will be great happiness to find in death the true life and respite from such great toil, it will be a great misfortune for those islands to lose their preachers, when they need them so much.

And so that this may be done most smoothly and with-out great cost, as would be the case with a garrison of Spaniards, their lack may be made up, if Your Majesty is pleased to so order, by sending 200 men from Manila, or the largest number possible of Indians[23] of the Philip-pines, of good character and old Christianity, like the Pampangos and Tagalog; for although they come without Spaniards, because of the scarcity of the latter in Manila and the greater expenses of their support in the Marianas Islands, these old Christians will be able to realize the said effect even without any other director than Captain Don Juan de Santa Cruz, who at present is head of the lay companions of the Fathers; and such could he be in any

[23] The Spanish used the word *indios* to refer to the indigenes both of the New World and of the Philippines and other Pacific island groups.

post of Your Majesty's, for his valor, Christianity, and the zeal with which he has served outstandingly in this mission, earning notable respect for the name of Christian and Spaniard amongst these natives, whose language and customs he knows well. And without him, some of the Pampangos Indians could serve as captain during the time when Your Majesty might not wish to put a regular garrison in these islands. In exchange for the Indians who might have come from Manila, you could send there the same number of Marianos, who will go with pleasure, as they already began to go in the past year of 1668; and it would be much easier, with this exchange and mixture of old and new Christians, to govern these lands; because in this way Christian customs will be introduced more easily and smoothly here, with the arrival at one and the same time of the words of the preachers and the examples of the old Christians. All of this is much easier to do in these islands than in others, because they are on the route of the Manila galleons.

3. They ask Your Majesty to give an urgent order that the galleons of regular support for the Philippines stop on their return from Acapulco in the harbor of San Antonio of the island of Guam, or in another of the known ones if it is deemed more convenient; and on the return from Manila have them stop at the harbor of San León, on the west of the island of Agrigan, which is fifteen leagues north of the one they call the Isle of the Volcanoes; and have them take account of the state of the Marianas Islands and carry out, when their offices are needed, punishment and remedy of whatever misfortunes might occur, bringing help to said people and whatever else Christian charity might suggest, especially clothing to dress our Lord Jesus Christ who is extremely naked in these poor Marianos, so that our Lord may say to them on the Day of Judgment: "I was naked and you clothed me." For the galleons to stop at said harbors would add no cost whatever, but rather, in addition to the convenience to the said ships of taking on water it might result in savings

of the expenses for the small ship that it has been necessary to send specially to the aid of these islands, although the latter should go from time to time, for the purposes that we shall describe.

4. They ask what was asked for last year: that a sufficient and suitable ship be sent from Manila without other charge than to reconnoiter the harbors that are said to be in these islands, some of which have been found by Captain Don Juan de Santa Cruz, as we said at the beginning; and especially to explore the islands that link the Marianas with the Philippines, as they say these continue to the south beyond the island of Mindanao; because if this route is found, it will be easier to govern and communicate with one and another island, for then it might be done in small vessels; without this route things are very difficult, because one cannot travel to the north [sic] except in high-sided and very strong ships, owing to the terribleness of the seas that lie between the Philippines and the Marianas. For this exploration, Captain Antonio de Acevedo seems very suitable; he came as principal pilot of the ship that brought the missionaries to the Marianas Islands and offered to undertake this exploration.

5. Because there can be no hesitation in matters of so great importance as the salvation of souls, redeemed by the Blood of Jesus Christ, we propose to Your Majesty with new urgency, greater than that which was held in the past because of the extreme necessity of so many souls being lost, that you be pleased to order that explorers go from Peru to the Austral land, previously unknown and the reputed fifth part of the world, and to the Solomon Islands and to the others in the South Sea that are mentioned in the voyage of Captain Pedro Fernández Quirós, and that continue from this island of Guam to very near Peru, as is mentioned in the account of that voyage that was referred to in the report of the previous year.[24]

[24] The geographical conceptions presented and implied in this section mirror quite faithfully the arguments of Quirós in his

6. To explore in particular the islands that link the Marianas with the islands of Japan, someone from New Spain could come with a ship brought from the ports of Guatemala, or brought from Peru to the port of Acapulco, as has occurred before in aid of the Philippines; there are not lacking people in Mexico who would make this voyage, as Don Antonio de Medina offered to do, and by their own means and wealth, or by the wealth of others whom Your Majesty might honor with some title or a grant in part of the land that they place under the rule of our Lord Jesus Christ and the Catholic Crown of the King our Lord; with ministers of the Holy Gospel they could probably more easily and with less expense to the royal treasury obtain a great increase and extension of our Holy Catholic Faith and the salvation of so many who are now deprived totally of salvation, the Lord having entrusted the task of conversion by the current arrangement to the royal and Catholic zeal of Your Majesty and most heedful Council, in whose prompt resoluteness depends today the great importance of cultivating said lands and introducing the Faith into them now, when it is most easy, because they are yet free of Mohammedans, heretics, and other pestilential sects.

7. We request Your Majesty be pleased to establish a seminary in the island of Guam for the good instruction of the boys of this land, orphans by nature or custom of this nation, in which sons are totally free from education

famous and widely translated *Eighth Memorial*; many contemporaneous translations of the latter have been reproduced in a most valuable work of Carlos Sanz, *Australia: Su Descubrimiento y Denominación* (Madrid, 1973). Interestingly, the first and other Spanish editions of the *Memorial* refer to the Austral land as the fourth part of the world, not the fifth, as it was referred to in languages other than Spanish. An excellent review of conjectures about, and discovery and exploration of, the Austral lands is in Colin Jack-Hinton, *The Search for the Islands of Solomon, 1567–1838* (Oxford, 1969).

and rule by their parents.[25] This barbarity will make it easier to introduce our care and to gather them into said seminary houses, opposing this sacred and royal seminary to those public houses the Devil has founded in these islands, *Urritaos* where youths live with unmarried women with no other control or direction than what the Devil or their appetite persuades them to, urged by the libertinage of their age. Until others are founded in the rest of the islands, we shall try to select for this seminary from all the islands the boys of greatest ability, best nature, and application to Christian doctrine, and they will be able later to serve as *Canacápoles* or teachers of the rest; and the most highly regarded can be ordained as priests, for the Marianos do not have drunkenness, which has been the principal impediment that those of other nations have had to receiving sacred orders. Saint Francis Xavier, the Apostle of the Indies, believed that the principal fruit of the Gospel was in the children, whose teaching and education he commended above all things to his companions; because Christianity, introduced in childhood, grows and grows as does age itself, and they are good Christians when men and old men who were Christians since childhood. The same Francis Xavier, when the governor of the East Indies assigned 4000 *pardaos*[26] that were part of the marriage gift of Queen Catalina of Portugal from the tributes of the fisheries, wrote to the queen and beseeched her to grant this gift, giving this reason: "For these Christian children, sons and grandsons of Gentiles, are, My Lady, the best marriage gifts with which Your Highness can best and most certainly enter into heaven." And we can say of this seminary for boys, whose establishment we

---

[25] Sanvítores also sent a memorial to the king concerning the seminary, and the queen, acting as regent, granted his request by edict of April 18, 1673, together with an annual grant for its support from the royal treasury in Mexico (Le Gobien, *Histoire des isles Marianes*, pp. 103–105).

[26] A coin of low value used by the Portuguese in Goa. *Enciclopedia Universal Ilustrada Europeo-Americana*, vol. 41, p. 1420.

hope from the royal munificence and piety of the Queen our Lady, that these Christian boys, sons and grandsons of infidels and barbarians, will be the best guard of the King our Lord, and this house the best castle and fortress of all your kingdoms.

If there were means, it would be very worthwhile to found also a seminary for girls of the Marianas, where they might be gathered before the Devil takes them for their *Urritaos* or public houses where youths live with maidens or unmarried girls, as we have said, whom they select and bring from one place to another with the obscene and infamous consent of their parents, who permit it by reason of their interest in the payment.

8. For the immediate administration and inspection of these islands, delayed so long and made so risky by reason of the frail craft of those [*sic*] islands, we need at least two boats in the form of launches that can be carried from the Philippines in the galleons, like others that the galleons often carry to Acapulco; and with these same ships it will be possible to leave people and aid that may be brought from the Philippines in aid of the Marianas with more ease and no hardship for the galleons, when there might be contrary winds, which they are accustomed to experiencing when coming from Manila.

These things the preachers of the Gospel of the Marianas Islands ask for and request of Your Catholic Majesty for the propagation and increase there of our Holy Faith. This the most blessed martyr Luis de Medina asks from heaven, and he signed these chapters and requests with his hand and has since confirmed them with his blood, spilled for Christ. We rest our hope in Divine and Royal Providence, that these so just desires will be fulfilled, addressed only to the greater glory of God and the good of His souls, for God and His Vicar have commended these islands to the King our Lord and the Queen our Lady that they may bring to them His Gospel; in which one sees how much the Lord loves them and desires their eternal happiness. It is well known how in the new spiritual conquest of the Marianas Islands, ordered by the King our Lord Philip the Fourth (who is now in heaven) and carried on now by our King Charles the Second and the Queen our Lady, they surpassed the great zeal of all the kings before them, for whereas some in the East Indies and others in the West introduced the Gospel and carried the Faith to some lands where they might find gold, silver, precious stones, and other things of great value and esteem, our most Catholic kings have carried the Faith to some islands where there is nothing more than some souls redeemed by the Blood of Jesus Christ (more precious in His eyes than heaven and earth), without searching in them for more than the glory of God; although with this they will gain everything, for Jesus Christ says: "Seek first the kingdom of heaven, and His justice, and you shall find all these things." May our small[27] and great monarch live many centuries, so that, opening many doors to the Gospel, he shall open as many more to the blessings of his far-flung empire. It is an auspicious horoscope of his blessings to have begun to preach the Faith in the Marianas Islands in his reign, during which heaven promises that our king shall be conqueror of many kingdoms, no less for Jesus Christ than for his royal crown. So be it. So be it.

[27] Charles II was born in 1661 and hence was ten years old at the time the pamphlet was published.

*Epilogue*

n 1968, three centuries after the Jesuit missionaries landed in the Marianas and some two decades after its devastating involvement in a major war, Guam had a population of about 100,000, of whom more than a third were associated with the military forces of the United States. Only 252 persons called themselves full-time farmers, and they cultivated only about one percent of the land. No animals were raised commercially. The underdeveloped state of agriculture on Guam was partly owing to uncertainty about land tenure because of destruction of records and landmarks in the heavy fighting of the Second World War, and partly the result of ownership by the military and the local government of about two-thirds of the land, a circumstance that has removed much of it from agricultural use.[1] The conse-

[1] David Lee, "Problems in Tropical Agriculture: A Case Study of Guam," *Yearbook of the Association of Pacific Coast Geographers*, vol. 33 (1971), pp. 46–64, at pp. 46, 48, 57; "Bombers and Bikinis," *Wall Street Journal*, October 23, 1973, p. 40. In a sense, dependence on importation of food began with the establishment of the mission; one of the early missionaries wrote that "to sustain life they had to bring plants and seeds and animals from elsewhere." Luis Morales, "Dos Relaciones adjuntas del estado y progressos que desde el año de 1681 tienen aquellas Islas [Marianas]," Newberry Library, Ayer Collection ms. 1391.

quent dependence on imports of food is extreme even for subtropical islands, many of which share Guam's need for food imports, and it contrasts sharply with conditions of three centuries ago, when the Marianos, like their ancestors who thought they were the only people in the world, were self-sufficient through necessity. In addition, by 1973, as much as one-quarter of the work force had to be imported to meet the labor demands of the military and tourists. The latter are mostly Japanese, and they come to Guam because of its location and political affiliation: it is the closest American territory to Japan, whose citizens like to have American visas in their passports; some couples are said to delay their weddings until they arrive in Guam, so they can be married on American soil.[2]

Military interest in Guam also continues to be based upon its location, however altered by technological changes may be the strategic and geopolitical considerations that made the island valuable when the United States assumed control of it after the Spanish-American War. For some, Guam retains the strategic importance assigned to it by Sanvítores: in a general sense, it continues to be seen as a highly important base of operations for the West in light of the traditionally uneasy relationship between East and West that both preceded and has outlasted his day. Because of its location astride and near the end of the only westward route of colonial times that linked Europe and the Far East, even though only indirectly through Manila, Guam seemed to have been assured of continuing contact with both major terminals of the route. Sanvítores thought it capable for this reason of playing the central role in religious and imperial operations that were to fan out along his archipelago of San Lázaro in the western Pacific, a chain of islands that he believed to stretch nearly to Peru. Had his dream been realized, Pacific island societies would be very different

[2] "Bombers and Bikinis," *Wall Street Journal*, October 23, 1973, p. 40.

today, because of the fundamental differences between Spanish methods of colonization and those of other European nations. As things turned out, of all these societies only the Marianos felt the full and devastating, but unintended, impact of Spanish imperialism, wherein Church and State worked together to establish in exotic societies a semblance of Western ways.

The essence of the Spanish method was to support missionary activities with a "paternal but also coercive and military" justice and government, if circumstances required the latter; that is, the missionary effort assumed primacy in a joint venture, and we have seen that the occupation of the Marianas occurred at the instigation of a priest, Sanvítores, and not the authorities of the Philippines, who opposed it.[3] After initial reconnaissances by the Spanish in which the dimensions of colonizing problems were gauged by census taking and a search for leaders, and in which preaching and conversion were also important and the presence of military authorities might be helpful, the second step was often taken of altering the pattern of settlement from one of many dispersed hamlets to a wholly different one of large towns that facilitated the offering of religious services to the public. Thus in Guam, by the early 1680s, seven large villages with churches had replaced the more than 160 hamlets that had been counted at the beginning of the mission in 1668; the population of Rota had been congregated into two large villages. In addition, Agana had been distinguished from the other centers by the concentration of Spanish power there: it had a wooden fort enclosing a large, new church, a new house for the governor (a hurricane and fire had destroyed the earlier buildings), and a hospital for the soldiers. Agana had been selected as the principal cluster because of the advantages

[3] In an attempt to restrain the military, Sanvítores emphasized to the soldiers that they had come to convert the people, not to conquer them. Le Gobien, *Histoire des isles Marianes*, p. 147.

of its harbor and its traditional importance to the Marianos.[4]

The policy of congregation had been developed and widely applied in the Spanish possessions of the New World and was easily transferred to the Marianos. Conventional, also, was the establishment of a garrison where necessary and feasible, as well as a complete system of local government derived from Spanish practice and supervised by Spanish officials: Marianos were governed directly by their fellow Marianos, most of them appointed by the governor and captain general of the islands.[5] He chose captains, lieutenants, and sheriffs (*alguaciles*); the Jesuits appointed the *fiscales*, who recorded births and deaths.

Clearly, much in these joint ventures depended on the character of the governor and his willingness to cooperate with the missionaries, who were naturally very much concerned about his selection. In practice, hardly any of the early governors were regarded as wholly satisfactory by the missionaries, especially where their behavior toward the Marianos was concerned, nor did the governors have very good relationships with all their underlings. This unfortunate situation was understandable, since the good, old Christians of exemplary behavior whom the mission-

〰〰〰〰〰〰〰〰〰〰〰〰〰〰〰〰〰〰〰〰〰〰〰〰〰〰〰〰〰〰〰〰〰〰〰〰〰〰〰〰〰〰〰〰〰〰〰〰〰〰〰〰

[4] Morales, "Dos Relaciones . . ."

[5] For similar examples from Mexico, see Mario Hernández Sánchez-Barba, *La Ultima Expansión Española en América* (Madrid, 1957), who discusses late eighteenth-century military and religious policies in northwestern Mexico and the Pacific coastal region of North America; and, of the many works by Peter Masten Dunne, S.J., *Pioneer Jesuits in Northern Mexico* (Berkeley and Los Angeles, 1944). The results of Spanish missionary and military efforts in the Philippines are described by John Leddy Phelan, *The Hispanization of the Philippines* (Madison, 1967). The very different outcome of attempts by missionaries and other Spaniards to penetrate Japan, a principal goal, is dealt with by Lothar Knauth, *Confrontación Transpacífica: El Japón y el Nuevo Mundo Hispánico* (Mexico City, 1972); in the cases of both the Philippines and Japan, as with the Marianas, the direct links with Mexico were of great importance.

aries had hoped for did not arrive in numbers sufficient to overcome the disorderly influence of the soldiers, many of whom were involuntary residents of the islands.[6] Thus, in 1682, the head of the mission wrote to the Duchess of Aveiro asking her to find a good governor for the islands, because if the head of government was unsatisfactory the soldiers would amount to little or nothing, or even harm the enterprise.[7]

The governor was of dual importance to the missionaries: besides being the head of the garrison, he was also the supreme magistrate of the Marianas, in a position to dispense harsh and summary justice. Antonio de Sarabia, governor and captain general in the early 1680s, probably was not unique in the severity of his sentences: three soldiers who had disobeyed his order not to commit rape were garroted on the spot where their crime was committed; two Marianos, brought in by some of their fellows as participants in the killing of two missionaries, were drawn and quartered. Sarabia, an unmarried man subject to seizures (*achaques*), puritanical, deeply religious and in intent a lay missionary, was greatly offended by what he regarded as the gross and obscene sensuality of the Marianos, and abhorred their "loose talk" with women. His predecessor, Joseph de Quiroga, who had been encouraged to go to the Marianas by the duchess, had been more satisfactory but was too much inclined to meddle in things spiritual and too much governed by fixed ideas.[8] Indispensable though the governors came to be to the

[6] The head of the mission wrote to Father García in 1681 that the soldiers did a great deal of harm, especially those who had been exiled to the Philippines from Mexico. He characterized them as *gente pícara*, "rascally knaves." Newberry Library, Ayer Collection ms. 1436.

[7] In his earlier letter to García, the head of the mission had written that if anything was to be obtained from the king, it would have to be with the help of the duchess, who had made the mission's business her own. *Ibid.*

[8] *Ibid.*

missionaries, the relationships of the two parties were seldom as smooth as the latter preferred them to be.

In spite of inadequate and uneven support from the secular arm, the head of the mission, Luis Morales, could recite an impressive list of accomplishments in 1681, little more than a decade after its establishment. Under pain of death, the Marianos had been ordered to surrender their dangerous lances made of bone and appeared to have complied with the order on Guam, at least. All marriages were now made only in perpetuity and performed by a priest before witnesses, the old marriages that could be formed and dissolved at will having disappeared. There was claimed to be not even a memory of the houses in which many unmarried young men kept one or more females; these had all been burned down and not replaced. The Marianos went regularly to Mass, and "the great license with which they formerly abandoned themselves to the sins of the flesh" had been restrained. After learning to grow and spin cotton, many were able to make clothes to cover their customary nakedness, and the rest had developed at least sufficient modesty to wear leaves as coverings.[9]

These changes in the pattern of settlement and in political, family, and social life were only few among many, yet were in themselves fundamental, revolutionary, and rapid: they had occurred within less than fifteen years. Although our own age is often described as one of rapid change, probably few would care to argue that we have seen changes that can match these in scope, magnitude, and rapidity.[10] They had been achieved at great cost to both parties, and the enormous tensions they produced were about to exact further tolls. In 1684, three years after

[9] Morales, "Dos Relaciones . . ."

[10] In spite of the massive nature of these changes, Laura Thompson found many survivals of the Marianos culture present on Guam in the 1930s. Thompson, *Guam and Its People* (Princeton, 1947), *passim*, especially chapter 10, "Gods and Ghosts."

the optimistic report of Morales, warfare broke out again on Guam, consuming much of what remained. In July and August of 1684, five priests were killed, and another martyred in July 1685; four had been killed in the uprising of 1674–1676, bringing to twelve the list of martyrs that began with the deaths of Medina in 1670 and Sanvítores in 1672. The number of deaths made the Marianas mission for many years one of the most dangerous in the history of the Society of Jesus. The military government responded by devising a policy of moving all the people to three islands, Guam, Rota, and Saipan, the better to control them, and finally moved the population of the latter to the other two islands. Warfare then ceased and, "by the 1740's, paganism had been reduced to the vanishing point."[11]

At the same time the population had also been reduced nearly to a point of no return. From about 100,000 in 1668, it declined to about 4000 in 1742; except for 200 or 300 on Rota, all lived on Guam.[12] Even before the uprising of 1684–1686 there could not have been more than 6000 Marianos left on Guam, which in 1668 had a population of more than 30,000.[13] Although many of the inhabitants fled to the supposed safety of the other islands, where their troubles soon followed them, many also succumbed to disease, and others were killed in battle.

Sanvítores's dream had come true: the Marianos were now all Christians; but, unfortunately, nearly all the converts as well as those who resisted conversion had disappeared. Nor did the location of the islands any longer

---

[11] De la Costa, *The Jesuits in the Philippines*, pp. 456–457.

[12] Richard Walter, *Anson's Voyage around the World* (London, 1928), p. 319. In this work, disease and despondency are emphasized as major causes of death, and the inhabitants of Tinian were said to have been moved to Guam because of the fall in population there. P. 293.

[13] Morales, "Dos Relaciones . . ."; Le Gobien, *Histoire des isles Marianes*, p. 46.

have the strategic value that attracted him: this value had been their unique position in a very large ocean.[14] Without the context of a grand design that gave them locational value and importance, the Marianas became merely very distant places. They became as they were described in the eighteenth century: "The land is sterile, the sky melancholy; the wind and sea turn furious, fearsome, formidable. Only in some seasons is its aspect peaceable; the people are few, barbarous and untutored. No one leaves there; no one passes by, there is no news of the rest of the world, not even of that small corner of it."[15]

꠸꠸꠸꠸꠸꠸꠸꠸꠸꠸꠸꠸꠸꠸꠸꠸꠸꠸꠸꠸꠸꠸꠸꠸꠸꠸꠸꠸꠸꠸꠸꠸꠸꠸꠸꠸꠸꠸꠸꠸꠸꠸꠸꠸꠸꠸꠸꠸꠸꠸꠸꠸꠸꠸꠸꠸꠸꠸꠸꠸꠸꠸꠸꠸꠸꠸꠸꠸꠸꠸꠸

[14] The value of location was, of course, to be regained in the twentieth century. A recent report from the Marianas describing their role in American military strategy states that Saipan and Tinian "will probably join Guam as the great new naval-and-air force bastion in the western Pacific." Submarines equipped with nuclear missiles operate from the naval base there, and bombers carrying nuclear weapons fly from Andersen Air Force Base. More than two hundred new Navy houses were under construction in 1973. "Guam Key to Navy Strategy," *St. Paul Pioneer Press*, August 5, 1973, I:10.

[15] A quotation in Zambrano, *Diccionario Bio-bibliográfico de la Compañía de Jesús en México*, vol. 1 (1961), p. 481; the date and source are not given but it may be in Pedro Murillo Velarde, *Geographia Historica*, 10 vols. (Madrid, 1752), of which vol. 8 deals with the Philippines; or in Pedro Murillo Velarde, *Historia de la Provincia . . . de Philipinas* (Manila, 1749).

*Index*

59

This book is set in linotype Janson with the display headings in Goudy Oldstyle. It is printed on Warren's Oldstyle and bound in Elephant Hide cover paper. It was designed by Robert N. Taylor of the University of Minnesota Press. Typesetting, printing, and binding are by Napco Graphic Arts, Incorporated, New Berlin, Wisconsin. Of the limited edition of 650 copies this is copy

343